美しい情景イラストレーション
ファンタジー編
幻想的な風景を描くクリエイターズファイル

Beautiful Scenes from a Fantasy World:
Background Illustrations and Scenes from Anime and Manga Works

Beautiful Scenes from a Fantasy World

Background Illustrations and Scenes from Anime and Manga Works

©2017 PIE International

PIE International Inc.
2-32-4 Minami-Otsuka, Toshima-ku, Tokyo 170-0005 JAPAN
international@pie.co.jp
www.pie.co.jp/english

ISBN978-4-7562-4966-1 (Outside Japan)
Printed in Japan

はじめに

現実からは程遠い、空想の世界に
私たちはいつだって魅了されています。
そこには、私たちが日常で忘れかけた
夢のかけらがあるからかもしれません。
『美しい情景イラストレーション』第2弾となる本書では、
ファンタジーの世界を魅力的に描くクリエイターの方々と
その作品を紹介します。
第1弾と同様に、ただの風景に止まらない、
見る人を壮大なファンタジーの世界へ誘う
情景的なイラスト作品を収録しています。
ファンタジーと一言で言ってもそのジャンルはさまざまあり、
本書で紹介している作品の世界観も多岐に渡ります。
どれも私たちの想像力を掻き立て、
魅力的なストーリーが感じられる作品ばかりです。
神秘的な自然風景や空中・海中都市、高度な機械文明や建築物など、
目を見張る作品の数々をご覧ください。
最後になりましたが、本書を制作するにあたり、
ご協力いただいたクリエイターの皆様、
その他すべての方々に心よりお礼申し上げます。

パイ インターナショナル編集部

Preface

We're always fascinated by fantastical worlds
that seem to exist far away from our own.
The reason for that might be because in those worlds,
there still exists a small piece of the dreams
we've almost forgotten through the busyness of everyday life.
This book, the second *Everyday Scenes from Parallel World*, introduces creators
who illustrate fantasy worlds in captivating ways, and the works they produce.
Just as in the first book, this book focuses not simply on background scenery,
but rather scenery illustrations that seem to invite the viewer
to enter into their magnificent fantasy worlds.
But even within "fantasy" there are several different genres,
and the illustrations in this book touch on a variety of those.
Each one stirs our imagination and presents an absorbing story to us.
From mysterious natural scenery and cities both in the air
and underwater to technologically advanced civilizations and buildings;
feast your eyes upon the worlds shown here that are sure to amaze you.
Finally, we'd like to thank all the artists and everyone else
involved in helping to create this book.
Thank you.

PIE International Inc. Editorial Department

目　次　｜　Contents

本書の見方　|　Book Layout

作品掲載ページ
Works Page

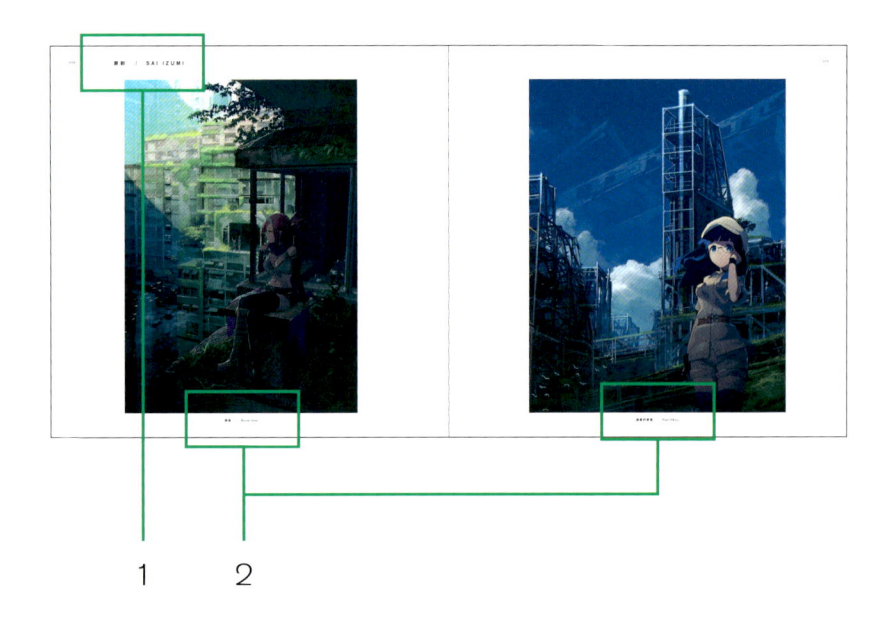

1　　2

プロフィール掲載ページ
Profile Page

泉 彩　|　SAI IZUMI

W : http://syakugan100.blog.fc2.com　**M :** syakugan100@gmail.com

P : 『メダロット ガールズミッション』（ロケットカンパニー）、『風雨来記3』（日本一ソフトウェア）キャラクターデザイン、『ロデア・ザ・スカイソルジャー』（角川ゲームス）パッケージ、イメージビジュアル他、ライトノベルやトレーディングカードゲーム、ソーシャルゲームなどのイラストを担当。
He has worked on character design for *Medarot Girls Mission* (Rocket Co.) and *Furaiki 3* (Nippon Ichi Software), and packaging and visuals for *RODEA THE SKY SOLDIER* (KADOKAWA GAMES), as well as illustrations for light novels, trading card games, social games, and more.

C : 絵を描いて生きています。泉彩と申します。マイペースで、いろいろな方々に助けられながら生きています。これからも頑張ります。
I live to draw. My name is Sai Izumi. I live my own way, being helped by many different people. I'll keep working hard in the future.

T : Photoshop CS5 / SAI

1　　　　　　　　　　　　　3　　2

---

1 : 作家名
Artist's name

2 : 作品タイトル
Work title

1 : ホームページやSNS等のアドレス、またはID、メールアドレス、
使用している制作ツール
Website or social media website address, as well as usernames,
email addresses, and tools used.

2 : 作家のプロフィール
Artist's profile

3 : 創作についてのコメントやメッセージ
Comments and messages regarding the creation process.

これからご紹介する作品は、32 名のクリエイターの方々による
美しい情景イラストの世界です。
自然物と人工物が共存する幻想的な景色、
ミステリアスな遺跡や建築物、
そして美しく魅惑的な世界観など、
無限に広がる空想の世界をお楽しみください。
また、クリエイターの方々と
本書を手に取ってくださった方々との架け橋になることを願い、
巻末にクリエイターの方々のプロフィール、
コメント等を掲載しております。

This book introduces the world of
beautiful scenery illustrations
from the work of 32 artists.
Enjoy endless worlds of fantasy with magical scenery
inhabited by both the natural and the manmade,
mysterious ruins and buildings, beautiful,
charming worlds and other such fantastic creations.
At the end of the book,
we've included a profile for
each artist along with comments
from the artists to try and bridge the gap
between viewer and artist.

休息　｜　Break time

過去の栄光　｜　Past Glory

道案内　|　Showing the way

階段 ｜ Steps

通学路　│　On the Way to School

旧市街 ｜ Old City District

花見 ｜ Gazing at Blossoms

夢常町の明楽さん　|　Akira of Mujo-cho

A g +

Bright Flight

Flutter Flyover

Fruiter of Track

Means More Than

旅路1　│　Journey 1

旅路2　│　Journey 2

旅路3 ｜ Journey 3

旅路4 ｜ Journey 4

捕らわれていた特殊な力を持つ少女。隙を見て逃げ出した少女は、
見知らぬ街（ほとんど廃墟）に辿り着く。
そこで敵の追撃と無理な加速でエンジンが故障し、
乗っていた飛行船が墜落するが、いち早く気づいた少年が間一髪、少女を救助する。
そんなめくるめく物語が待っている王道 SF ストーリーです（笑）。

A girl with special powers is captured. She waits for her chance then makes her escape,
only to find herself lost in a town of full of ancient ruins. As enemies pursue her, her airship's engine
breaks down under the excessive strain of acceleration as she tries to escape, sending it crashing toward
the ground. But a young boy who notices her plight manages to rescue her by a hair's breadth.
It's that kind of dazzling, but classic science fiction story (laughs).

rescue（線画）　|　rescue (Line drawing)

おさむらいさんアルバム『夢を見る意味 イラストジャケット盤』ジャケットイラスト　|　CD jacket illustration for the Osamuraisan album *Yume wo Miru Imi, Illustrated Jacket Edition*

そらる×まふまふ1st メジャーアルバム『After the Rain クロクレストストーリー 通常盤』(NBC ユニバーサル・エンターテイメントジャパン)ジャケットイラスト
CD jacket illustration for Soraru X Mafumafu 1st Major Album *After the Rain Kurokuresuto Sutori, Normal Edition* (NBC Universal Entertainment Japan)

磯撫での魍寮（線画） | Spirit Dorm where the *Isonade* Resides (Line drawing)

「磯撫で」という鯨のような巨大な妖怪が住まう海の上には、橋のように架かっている
学寮があります。そんな変わった場所には人間として生きる妖怪たちが人間の真似を
するように勉学に励んでいる、その日常を描きました。それでもやっぱり思いがけない
ことを起こしそうで、危うくて……と、想像すると楽しそうだと思い描かせて
いただきました。景色を見渡せる大きな窓からは磯撫でがジャンプしています。

There's a dormitory that looks like a bridge stretching across the sea where the *Isonade* – a giant whale – like spirit – resides.
In that strange place, the spirits that live like humans appear to be imitating them by studying. I drew a picture of
what an everyday scene in that world would look like. But in the picture there's also the sense something unexpected might happen,
something dangerous… that's what I thought. Imagining stuff like this is fun for me, and I tried to put that into my work.
From the big scenic window you can see the *Isonade* jumping.

tropical rium

申年の大晦日 | New Year's Eve in the Year of the Monkey

酉の杜 | A Forest of Birds

じめじめ日和 ｜ Lovely Weather if You Like It Damp

Underwater Symphony

黒須ノカ | Noka Kurosu

Screen

無題 | Untitled

アストルア | Astrolua

紺碧　|　Azure

白の塔　|　The White Tower

メルナイラ | Melnira

K,Kanehira

船頂から見下ろせば 星船が丘六丁目　｜　Looking Down from Atop a Ship on Hoshifunegaoka 6-chome

大遺跡村大字穴底　│　From the Bottom of a Hole in Big Ancient Ruins

魔法工城　|　The Magic Factory

雲くじらの住む街　|　Where the Cloud Whales Live

海中庭園　｜　Garden Under the Sea

エソラニア | Esorania

Kenta Doi

雲の都市　｜　City in the Clouds

西の塔 ｜ West Tower

ツリーハウス　|　Treehouses

宮 | Palace

華風 | Flowers in the Wind

希望のアドヴァンス　│　Hope's Advance

悠禮フルール　|　Ethereal Flowers All Aglow

夏の夢雲 ｜ Summer Dreams in the Clouds

Hidden City

Cave Exploration

Sunset

Steampunk City

機械じかけの渡り鳥　|　Migratory Birds Fly by the Machine

つばさ ｜ Wings

Amazing Grace

時の眠り　|　Time Sleeps Here

Anti-GravityCity ©JohnHathway

ElectricLolita ©JohnHathway

新体験型ゲームアプリ『真空管ドールズ』(ソニー・ミュージックエンタテインメント)イメージイラスト「空区 お空場」
Osora-ba, Sora-ku - Image illustration for the innovative game *Shinkukan Dolls* (Sony Music Entertainment)　©JohnHathway

旧秋葉原駅前　│　In Front of Old Akihabara Station　©JohnHathway

shirakaba

蜘蛛の糸 | Spider Web

索道都市 | City Suspended on a Cable

海月 | Jellyfish

竜宮の庭 | Garden of the Dragon's Palace

一休み | Taking a Break

お忍びの旅 | Journey Under a Hidden Identity

幻想の森 ｜ Forest of Illusions

霧の中 | In the Mist

燈火の空 | Lantern-lit Sky

2016.5.22 禅助.

あの日の私 | Me on That Day Long Ago

Soraizumi

Voice of Attribute

Alice the Interceptor

巨大サンゴの柱 ｜ Giant Coral Pillar

天空の街 ｜ District in the Sky

巨大サンゴの谷 ｜ Giant Coral Valley

巨大サンゴの街 ｜ Giant Coral Street

hope

desert city

壊れかけた世界 ｜ A World that is Almost Broken

空の旅 ｜ Journey Through the Sky

新緑廃工場 ｜ Abandoned Factory Overflowing with Green

空遺跡 ｜ Ruins in the Air

無味乾村 | Dry Town

配管工事　│　Pipes Under Construction

Hunt_01-02

辺境市街 | Town on the Edge of the Frontier

飛翔 ｜ Soaring

妖亭 | The Bewitching Manor

この街は俺たちが守る！　｜　We'll Protect this Area!

巨大建築郡　｜　Huge Building District

寝室にて　｜　In the Bedchamber

遺跡都市　｜　Town of Ancient Ruins

商店通り　|　Shopping District

空の見える茶館　|　Teahouse with a View of the Sky

きのこ狩り　｜　Mushroom Picking

2017年賀絵　New Year's Card Illustration for 2017

旅立ちの朝 ｜ The Morning of Departure

ひとやすみ ｜ A Quick Rest

藤木ゆう ｜ Yu Fujiki

時の管理人さん ｜ The Timekeeper

yucat 2ndアルバム『PARALLEL WORLD Ⅱ〜第３ノ道〜』（つばさレコーズ）ジャケットイラスト | Jacket illustration for yucat's second album, *PARALLEL WORLD II – Dai 3 no Michi* (Tsubasa Records)

『Let's Make ★ Character CGイラストテクニックvol.7』（ビー・エヌ・エヌ新社）掲載イラスト
Illustration for *Let's Make ★ Character CG Illustration Technique vol.7* (BNN, Inc.)

GC ノベルズ『賢者の弟子を名乗る賢者 5』（マイクロマガジン社）カバーイラスト
Cover illustration for GC Novels *Kenja no Deshi wo Nanoru Kenja 5* (Micro Magazine Publishing Company)

天の御川に金魚を流し ｜ Releasing Goldfish to the Milky Way

妖怪商店街 | Downtown Where the Spirits Shop

時計の墓　｜　Grave of the Clock tower

故郷 | Old Hometown

階段 ｜ Stairway

旅立ち ｜ Setting Off

夜桜　｜　Cherry Blossoms at Night

煌夜 | Dazzling Night

酉　|　The Bird

魔物居住域　|　Where the Spirits Dwell

森の家　|　House in the Woods

不思議の街 | A Street Steeped in Mystery

森の村　|　Village in the Forest

Sky home

「出陣式」『「ファンタジー背景」描き方教室』（SB クリエイティブ）掲載イラスト
Sending Off Ceremony – Illustration for *'Fantaji Haikei' Kakikata Kyoushitsu* (SB Creative)

野営 ｜ Camping Out

天想 ｜ Feelings in the Sky

星渡りの旅団　│　A Journey Across Stars

潜思科学機構五号 | Deep Scientific Thought Machine Number Five

蒼の摩天楼 | Blue Skyscrapers

Temple Memories（線画）　｜　Temple Memories(Line drawing)

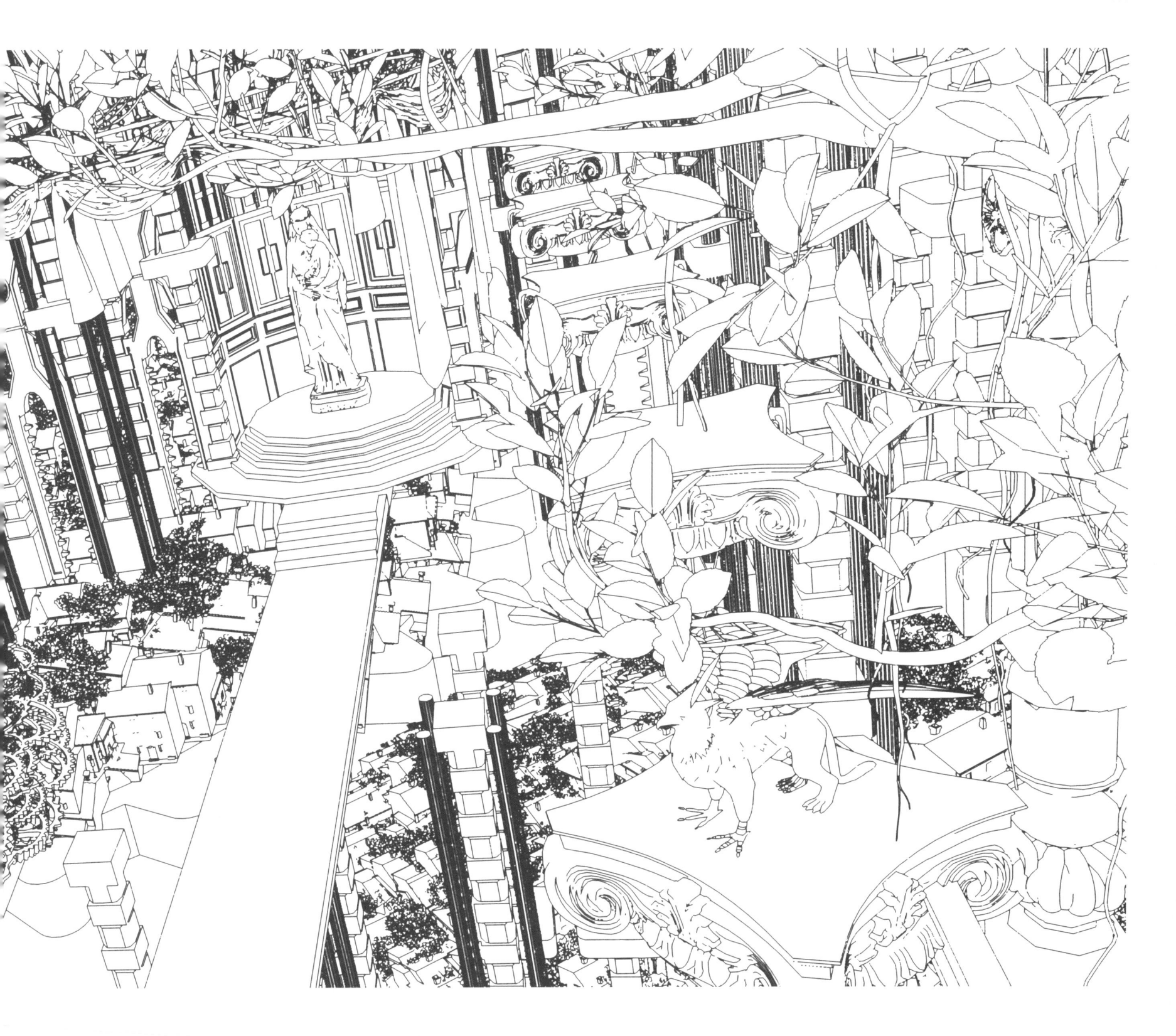

空中都市に住まう人々の象徴的な存在となっている神殿。太陽により近い場所に浮遊する神殿には、陽の光が力強く降り注いでいます。今作では空気の薄さを表現するために、特にライティングや陰影のコントラストに気を遣いました。

For the people who live in this city in the sky, the temple shown here has a symbolic significance. Because the temple floats close to the sun, strong sunlight shines down on the scene. I paid special attention to the lighting, specifically the contrast between light and shadow in order to express how thin the air is there.

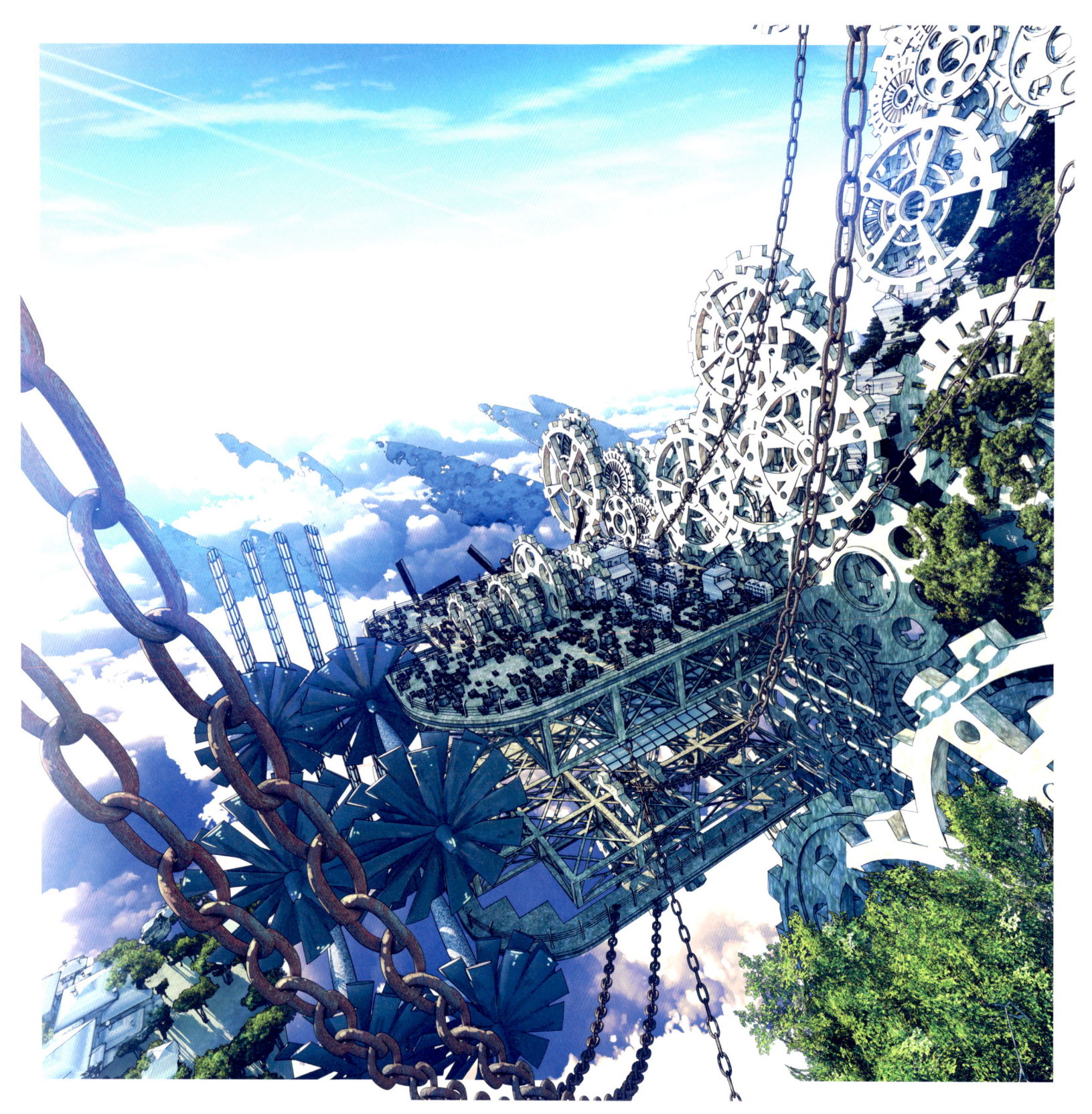

AEROPOLIS

GEARS

TERRAFORMING

光の街の秘密 | Secret of the City of Light

カバーイラストメイキング

Showcase of the cover illustration process

オーバーテクノロジーと大自然とが融合したドラマチックな世界。
イラストレーター、コンセプトアーティストのよー清水さんに
魅力的なファンタジーイラストと
その世界観の作り方についてお聞きしました。

A dramatic world created through the combination of
futuristic technology and Mother Nature.
We asked Yo Shimizu, an illustrator and concept artist,
how he designed this captivating fantasy illustration and about its setting.

1 : [言葉からラフを起こす | Draw rough drafts inspired by ideas]

ラフ1

ラフ2

まず、どのような絵にしたいのかを書き出します。

・シリーズ2冊目のカバーイラストなので、1冊目とは異なるイメージにすること。
・ファンタジーの壮大さ、ワクワク感を重視すること。
・絵を描く以上にひとつの世界観を作ることを意識すること。

これら3つの要件を頭に叩き込み、ラフを数枚作成します。1冊目と異なるイメージということで曲線を多用し、ファンタジーのワクワク感は王道の浮遊都市で、世界観の作り込みはゲームや映画のコンセプトアートを作る過程を再現することで表現しようと考えました。
絵を描く時に最も大切なのは、何を伝えたいか、狙いをしっかりと定めることです。
伝えたい事がない絵はクオリティが高くても、見る人の心を動かせません。
今回は書籍名の「美しい」という言葉に合うような奥行きと安定感のあるラフ1で進行することになりました。

First, I listed up ideas about what kind of illustration I wanted to create; for example:

・My job is to design the cover of the second book in a series,
　so I need to create an illustration that is different from the look of the first book.
・I have to understand the importance of establishing a grand world of fantasy
　that gives viewers lots of excitement.
・I also must pay attention to creating a particular setting rather than just putting all my efforts into drawing.

I told myself to get my head around these three points, and then created a few drafts. I used many curved lines to make objects appear different from those in the first cover. I was also thinking that I would try to foster a sense of excitement by drawing a floating city—a classic fantasy element, and to shape this world's setting by replicating the process of designing concept arts for games and films.
The most important thing when drawing a picture is to nail down what you want to say through your drawing. A well-crafted illustration without the author's message will not move or inspire viewers.
Out of two drafts I created, we finally chose to go forward with the first draft because it had depth and a sense of stability that was suitable for the word "beauty," which is in the Japanese title of the book.

2 : [世界観を決める | Establish a setting]

ラフはあくまで初見のカッコよさを重視して作成したので、私がよく使う表現や手癖が多いです。ここから新しい世界観を作るために、各要素のイメージや設定を書き出したり、スケッチを繰り返しながら決めていきます。

When creating the drafts, I kept in mind the need to make them look stylish for eyes that were viewing them for the first time, so they were mostly made based upon my recurring expressions and drawing habits. In order to conceive a brand new setting, I had to jot down ideas for all the elements and contexts, and express their appearance in sketches. These gradually began to take form after many attempts.

背景本　表紙

大地は毒で汚染され、人々が空に逃れた世界
技術は失われ産業革命期のレベルまで落ちている。一部で過去の遺物を使ったオーバーテクノロジーが使われているレベル

自然とメカ→　羽虫＋メカ

飛行機械はロマンだよな！

ファンタジー感なら浮遊大陸　オーバーテクノロジー　超古代文明　幾何学デザイン

一冊目の表紙との差　曲線　自然を模した曲線多めの建物

建築素材は石と木

虫や動物を模した機械
.....羽虫、トンボ、蜘蛛、蝶、

古代生物デザイン？　巨大トンボ、

カンブリア紀　バージェス動物群

The cover for the background illustration book

In the world of the illustration, the ground is covered in toxins, and humans have fled to the sky.
Technology has now fallen back to a pre-Industrial Revolution level, but some futuristic technologies made from relics of the past still exist in this world.

Nature and machines -> Flying insects and machines

Flying machines make me imagine a great future!

A floating city for a fantasy feel Futuristic technologies Ancient civilizations Geometric designs

Be different from the first cover Curves Buildings with many curved lines inspired by nature

Buildings are made of stone and wood

Machinery that looks like insects and animals

Flying insects, dragonflies, spiders, butterflies, etc.

Designs of ancient creatures? Giant dragonflies

The Cambrian period The Burgess Shale fauna

飛行機械が発達した世界というイメージが最初からあったので、資料を元に飛行機械のスケッチから始めます。魅力的なデザインには明確なテーマがあるので、見ただけで用途や動きを想像できます。今回はバージェス動物群という、約５億年前に生息したといわれている奇妙な古生物達をテーマにしました。
また、この世界観に合う植物をデザインしたいと考えました。映画やゲームの世界観を作るというテーマなので、植物のデザインは植物に詳しいイラストレーターに制作してもらいました。近年の大規模なコンテンツでは、一人で全てのデザインを担当するのは物理的に不可能なので、複数人で制作をすることが多いです。魅力的で奥深い世界観は、さまざまな人のアイデアが集合して作られています。

From the beginning, I imagined the setting to be a world where aircraft had developed further, so I began sketching flying machines based on reference materials. Attractive designs always have a clear theme, which lets an audience imagine how they move and how they are used just by looking at them. This time, I took my inspiration from the Burgess Shale fauna, unique ancient creatures that are said to have existed on Earth about five hundred million years ago.
I also wanted to design plants that fitted the setting. Because I was creating my illustration by replicating the process of creating a setting for games and films, I asked another illustrator who is more knowledgeable about plants, to produce some plant designs. In recent years, when working on large projects, it is physically impossible for one person to design all the elements, so nowadays many illustrators are involved in making one piece of work. A dazzling and complicated setting is often achieved by combining ideas from many people.

3:[素材を使って情報量を高める | Add more texture by using materials]

アナログ絵とデジタル絵の一番の違いは作品の情報量です。アナログ絵は紙のザラザラ感、絵の具のにじみ、量感など、莫大な情報を持っていますが、デジタル絵は単なるピクセルしかありません。制作時間があるときは情報量を描き込みで表現できますが、スピーディーに絵を仕上げたいときは、写真を使って絵の情報量を高めます。

ラフに写真をオーバーレイで重ねます。油彩などでキャンバスにあらかじめ絵の具を塗る下地作りのようなものですね。

ただし、写真を使う時は著作権に十分気をつけましょう。必ず著作権フリーのものか確認してから利用してください。

The biggest difference between analog and digital paintings lies in the amount of information they carry. Analog pictures have a large amount of information such as the texture of the paper, the weight of the ink, and the ink bleed, but digital illustrations are merely made of pixels. When you have plenty of time to work on a project, you can add texture by adding lines and paints, but when you want to speed up the process, you can use photos to add more texture to your illustration.

First, I suggest overlaying photos on the rough draft. This process is similar to painting a base layer in oil painting on canvas.

Be aware of and take care regarding copyright when using photos. Make sure you only use royalty-free materials.

4 : [重要な部分から描き始める | Start drawing the most important parts]

重要な部分から仕上げるのが効率的なので、まずは表紙部分から描き進めます。

新規レイヤーを作成し、表紙以外は黒で塗りつぶして、描くべきところに集中できるようにします。

建物の影となる部分に、空の色に近い鮮やかなブルーを使用して、全体的に爽やかな空気感を作りました。さらに、デザインした飛行機械や植物を描き込みます。

この辺で世界観が固まってきました。「古代文明の遺跡を鉱山のように発掘して、発掘品から機械を作り生活している世界」です。住人は遺跡に寄り添うように暮らしている、という設定です。

Start drawing the part that is going to be the cover first as it is most efficient to prioritize this area.

Create a new layer and paint the other parts in black temporarily, so that we can focus on the smaller section we are drawing.

I used a bright blue color similar to the color of the sky in the shadow of the buildings to create a light and cheerful atmosphere. Then, I added aircraft and plants that have already been designed.

By doing so, the setting became more visible. What I am trying to create is a world where people dig up relics of an ancient civilization — just like mining — and build machinery out of the excavated objects for a living. In this setting, people are living closely to the ruins.

5: [完成後をイメージする ｜ Imagine how the final illustration will be used]

表紙に入れる要素が大体決まったので、仕上がりの確認をします。カバーの
レイアウトを表示して、絵の要素が不自然に見えないか確認します。
キャラクターが帯で切れてしまいそうなので、近景を全体的に上げました。
このように、仕上がりの確認や媒体に合わせた要素の配置はとても大切です。
個人制作の場合でも一旦作品を俯瞰してみると、満足のいく仕上がりになる
と思います。

Now that we know what to incorporate in the cover, let's think about how it will look as a finished product.
I superimposed the design layout to make sure everything in the illustration appears as I intended.
Then I realized that the character might get cut off by the belly band around the book, so I moved the foreground elements up a little. It is very important to consider the placement of each element depending on the medium and its finish.
Even for a personal project, take one step back and comprehensively consider the overall look. That will let you achieve an illustration you can be happy with.

6 : [視線が集中する部分を描き込む │ Draw the part that catches most attention]

最も視線が集中する表紙の遠景部分を描き込みます。どこから描くかは人それぞれですが、よく見られる部分から描くことで絵の方向性を決めることができますし、仕上がりも速くなります。

当初の建築のイメージは古代遺跡というより、赤い屋根の宮殿のようだったので、流線型のつるりとした、少し未来的な雰囲気に変えます。

I started drawing the background illustration in the area that will become the cover because people's eyes move there first. It varies according to the illustrator as to which part to draw first, but by drawing the most-viewed part first, the artist can understand the overall direction of the picture, which speeds up the drawing process. The initial image I had for the buildings was of a red-roofed palace complex rather than an ancient ruin, so I changed them to curvy, smooth, and more futuristic structures.

POINT

人間は絵を点、またはエリアで見ます。例えばキャラクターのイラストであれば、まず顔の目の周辺を見ます。他にも「顔」「人物」「コントラストが高い部分」「明るい部分」を見るといわれています。極端に言えば、この部分さえしっかりと描いておけば、その絵を良い絵と認識してくれます。

When looking at a picture, people tend to focus on specific parts or areas. For example, if they are looking at an illustration of a character, they are drawn to the area around the eyes first. In addition to the eyes, people tend to pay attention to the character's face, the character as a whole, high-contrast areas, and bright sections. To speak of extremes, if you can draw these areas well, the viewers will acknowledge the whole picture as being well drawn.

7 : [色のバランスを確認する │ Check color balance]

色の情報が足りないと感じたので、以前描いたイラストをオーバーレイで重ねます。このように、自分の作品を合わせていくことで色の情報を追加することができます。写真や自分で描いたイラストを素材として上手く利用すれば、自分の発想にはない色が生まれ、ただ描いているだけでは起こりにくい偶然を作り出すことができます。こうして作った色は、手動で選んだ色より豊かで真似しにくいものになります。

I felt that this illustration needed more color information, so I overlaid my old illustration on it. You can add more colors by combining your current project with older drawings.
Utilizing photos and other illustrations you drew produces unimaginable colors and creates impressive coincidences that rarely occur when you simply draw. The colors created through this process are richer and more difficult to imitate than manually selected colors.

8 : [街を描く | Draw the cityscape]

まず、夜景の写真から作成した夜景ブラシを建物の影に使い、家から漏れる明かりを描きます。次に滝や森、煙を描き足し、全体の雰囲気を整えてから、民家の影をざっくりと描きます。
このように雰囲気を捉えてから形を取っていく方が自然に見え、しかも効率よく表現することができます。

I created a brush from a night-view photo and used it to draw the shadows of the buildings, and then I added the light escaping through the windows of houses. Next, I drew the forest, waterfalls and smoke, and then roughly sketched out the frames of the houses after checking and adjusting the overall atmosphere.
By grasping the overall atmosphere first, the final touch becomes more natural and the process more efficient.

9 : [ワクワク感を出す | Create excitement]

表紙部分を見て、全体にワクワク感が足りないことが気になりました。ワクワク感というのは感覚的なものですが、絵を見た時の率直な感想も大切です。そこで新規レイヤーを作成し、飛行機械をたくさん配置しました。たくさんのものが空に飛んでいるというのは、それだけでワクワクするものです。
思いついたアイデアやイメージは、新規レイヤーにどんどん描いてみましょう。デジタル絵はアナログ絵と違い、失敗してもそのレイヤーを非表示、削除すればすぐに元に戻せるので、悩むくらいなら描いてから考えることをおすすめします。

I felt that the cover, when looked at by itself, was failing to transmit a feeling of great excitement to viewers. Excitement is a subjective feeling, but I regard the first honest impression as being very important, so I added a new layer and added in a lot of aircraft. Seeing a great number of machines flying by excites us.
Add new layers and keep drawing whatever comes to mind. Unlike an analog painting, you can hide or delete layers if you make mistakes in the digital world. I urge you to go ahead and draw before you stop and wonder if you should.

10: [キャラクターとストーリーに深みを出す ｜ Add depth to characters and storylines]

キャラクターがぽつんといるだけで寂しげな雰囲気だったので、パートナーを追加しました。古代から動き続けているロボットです。デザインは建築と同じ曲線主体で、可動部は全て浮遊しています。キャラクターの雰囲気とデザインをさらにつかむため、簡単なスケッチを行います。この 2 人の関係性や、普段はどのように過ごしているのか、ストーリーのスケッチを一枚絵に落とし込みます。ロボットの不思議さを引き立てるために、女の子の年齢を下げました。

It looked lonely to see one character standing alone, so I added another character to accompany her. The new character is a robot that has existed since ancient times. The robot is designed the same as the buildings—with many curves—and all of his joints are floating in the air. In order to understand the feel of the characters deeper, and to develop my designs further, I drew rough sketches. I used these sketches to incorporate their stories, their relationships, and their daily lives into the illustration. To contrast the mysterious robot, I decided to make the girl appear younger.

11：[エフェクトを加える │ Add effects]

普通の一枚絵ではあまりみられない特殊効果を加えたいと思い、水滴とモーションブラー効果を加えることにしました。モーションブラーとは、高速で動く物体をカメラなどで撮影した時に、ぶれて見える現象です。絵に応用することでスピード感、臨場感を伝えることができます。モーションブラーは指先ツールにエアブラシを当てはめ、効果をかけたい部分を少しなぞるだけで簡単に表現できます。

I wanted to add special effects that are rarely seen in just one illustration, so I decided to use water droplets and motion blur. Motion blur is a blurring phenomenon that occurs when capturing fast-moving objects on a camera. Applying this effect to a drawing helps convey the feeling of speed and realism. It is easy to express motion blur by choosing airbrush on a smudge tool and lightly moving the cursor over the areas to which you want to add the effect.

水滴の効果は、キャラクターのストーリー性が少し弱いと思ったので加えました。当初はロボットが日傘をさしてあげているイメージでしたが、この時間では少し不自然です。そこで直前まで雨が降っていた事を伝えるために、カメラについた水滴を加えました。

I added water droplets because I felt the story of the characters as is was a little weak. Originally, the robot was holding a parasol over the girl, but it looked unnatural to do so at this time of the day. The water droplets, which appear as if they were on a camera lens, were used to express the fact it was raining until just a while ago.

POINT 性質の分解 | Analyzing the properties of the effects

水滴など特殊な表現は、資料を見ながら描くことはもちろんですが、それだけではなかなか表現できません。その場合は、まず「どうしてそう見えるのか?」を考え、性質を分解することで楽に描くことができます。

水滴の性質は「透明」「反射」「レンズ」です。透明は言葉の通り向こう側を描き、反射は光の方向を考えながら強いハイライトを入れ、レンズは水滴の際の部分に歪みをつけることで表現します。この考え方は、難しいモチーフやあらゆる表現で応用できます。

The first step when drawing special effects such as water droplets is to imitate good examples, but by doing that alone, it is difficult to accomplish realistic expressions. Analyzing why they look and appear as they do breaks down the properties of effects, which can help you draw them more easily.

The components that constitute a water drop are ansparency, reflection, and a lens. Transparency literally means that I can draw the background through the water. To create reflection, I added strong highlights, while taking into consideration where the light was coming from. A lens is expressed by distorting the edge of the water droplets. This analysis of properties can be used for any expression, including objects that are difficult to draw.

12 : [要素を仕上げる | Finishing all the elements]

シルエットで配置していた要素を、ひとつひとつ仕上げていきます。特に飛行機械はこの作品を印象付ける大切な要素なので、丁寧に描きます。

It is time to finish each of the components that have been drawn only as outlines. I paid extra attention to drawing the aircraft as they play an important role in determining the overall feel of this illustration.

遠くに見える飛行機械や建物はシルエットを整える程度にし、遠景と近景のメリハリをつけながら仕上げます。

I kept retouching to the minimum for the silhouettes of the flying machines and buildings seen in the distance so as to establish a clear difference between the foreground and the background.

近景の植物は、プロセス2で描いたデザイン画をよく見て特徴を抜き出しながら描き、画面に動きと楽しげなシルエットでワクワク感を演出します。最後に加算レイヤーを作成し、ポイントに発光表現を加えて完成です。

I referred to design sketches from the second process to understand the characteristics of the plants in the foreground so I could convey a sense of excitement through movement and fun shapes. Finally, I created an additional layer to add luminescent effects in certain areas, and voila, it was done.

飛行機械、キャラクター、植物など、ひとつひとつの要素を丁寧にデザインし、自分のできるいろいろな表現を取り入れてみました。また、メイキングはよくある「〜の描き方」というテクニック寄りのものより、ひとつの世界観の作り方、コンセプトワークの考え方に重点を置いて解説しました。

I drew intricate designs for each component such as aircraft, characters, and plants and tried to incorporate many of my own unique expressions. The behind-the-scene details of the drawing process are often described with a focus on techniques such as how to draw certain elements, but here I took a different approach by explaining in more detail about how to create a setting and conceptualize a work.

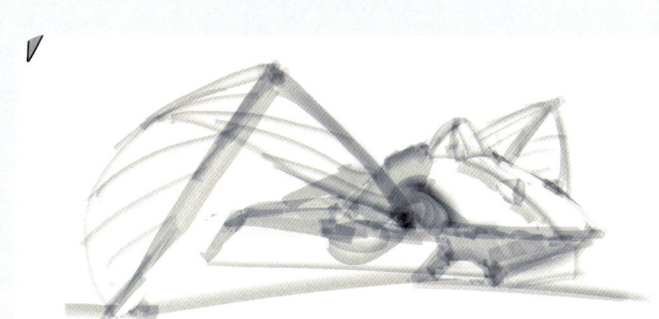

泉彩 ｜ SAI IZUMI

W：http://syakugan100.blog.fc2.com   **M**：syakugan100@gmail.com

P：『メダロット ガールズミッション』（ロケットカンパニー）、『風雨来記3』（日本一ソフトウェア）キャラクターデザイン、『ロデア・ザ・スカイソルジャー』（角川ゲームス）パッケージ、イメージビジュアル他、ライトノベルやトレーディングカードゲーム、ソーシャルゲームなどのイラストを担当。
He has worked on character design for *Medarot Girls Mission* (Rocket Co.) and *Furaiki 3* (Nippon Ichi Software), and packaging and visuals for *RODEA THE SKY SOLDIER* (KADOKAWA GAMES), as well as illustrations for light novels, trading card games, social games, and more.

C：絵を描いて生きています。泉彩と申します。マイペースで、いろいろな方々に助けられながら生きています。これからも頑張ります。
I live to draw. My name is Sai Izumi. I live my own way, being helped by many different people. I'll keep working hard in the future.

T： Photoshop CS5 / SAI

浮雲宇一 ｜ uiti

W：http://pikopicoufo.web.fc2.com   **M**：warauyurikago@gmail.com   **Tw**：@kumori_ufo

P：関西出身。1990（平成2）年の秋生まれ。趣味で絵を描いています。幻想的なものと黒髪の中性的な青年が好きです。主な活動は創作の同人イベントへの参加ですが、たまに書籍の装画等に関わらせていただいています。
Born in the fall of 1990 and hailing from the Kansai area of Japan. Draws pictures as a hobby. Likes include fantastical things and androgynous-looking young men with black hair. Most activities are related to participating in doujinshi (fan-produced manga) events, but also occasionally does book cover illustrations.

C：お楽しみいただけたなら幸いです。
I'd be really happy if you enjoyed my work.

T： Photoshop CS6 / SAI2

Ag+

M： atorieiji@gmail.com   **Tw**：@Atelieriji   **Pi**：900067

P：1986年10月19日生まれ。名古屋市出身、大阪市在住。ゲーム制作会社で3Dモデリングアーティストとして勤務する傍ら、趣味でイラストを描いており、SNS、デザインフェスタ、コミティアなどの場で作品を発表しています。
Born on October 19, 1986 in Nagoya. Currently resides in Osaka, Japan. Does 3D modeling for a video game company professionally and does illustration as a hobby. Displays works on SNS and at places like Design Festa and the COMITIA comic exhibition.

C：空に浮かぶ都市を舞台にした異世界の風景と、そこに暮らす人々の連作を描いているのですが、近頃はネタ切れ気味のため、訪れた場所や親しい知人をコッソリとモチーフにさせてもらっています。理想はあまり押しつけがましくない、自然と部屋に飾りたくなるような絵を描くことです！
Normally my illustrations all belong to a series based on an imaginary floating city, and I draw its scenery and the people who live there. But recently I've been getting the feeling I'm running out of original ideas, so I've taken to using the places I visited and the people around me as motifs for inspiration, secretly of course. I'm not aiming for anything in particular in my work. I just try to draw things that look good enough for people to want to hang up in their room!

T： Painter X3 / Photoshop CC2015 / コピックのミリペン / マーカー
Painter X3 / Photoshop CC2015 / Copic Multiliners / markers

S.kaz

W：http://kazuhiro-saito-s-kaz.tumblr.com   **M**：kazuhirosaito.illustration@gmail.com

P：1990年12月3日生まれ。福岡県出身。2016年2月に退職。フリーランスのイラストレーターとして活動中。
Born on December 3, 1990 and hailing from Fukuoka Prefecture, Japan. Retired from job in February 2016 and now does freelance work as an illustrator.

C：はじめまして。この度は私の作品をご覧いただきまして、誠にありがとうございます。こちらに掲載させていただきました作品は、どれも仕事の合間に描き進めていた作品です。皆さんに少しでも楽しんでいただければ幸いです。
Hello and thank you so much for taking a look at my illustration. The piece featured in this collection is one of several that I drew in my spare time while I was still working. I'd be very happy if you were entertained—even a little bit—by it.

T： Photoshop CC / Procreate

M.B

M：yo.draw.m.b@gmail.com   **Tw**：@yo_draw   **Pi**：6691409

P：9月7日生まれ。千葉県出身。CDジャケットイラスト、ソーシャルカードゲーム、書籍関連、グッズのデザイン制作など。ファンタジー絵を中心にいろいろ描きます。ボーカロイド・クリエイターのOrangestarと活動しています。
Born on September 7, in Chiba Prefecture, Japan. Has done illustrations for CD jacket covers, social card games, books, and has also worked on product designs. Illustrations cover a wide variety with a main focus on fantasy illustrations, and works closely with Vocaloid producer Orangestar.

C：今風の絵柄の中にも方向性を持って描いています。Orangestarとの活動の集大成、1stメジャーアルバム『未完成エイトビーツ』（Subcul-rise Record）、2ndメジャーアルバム『SEASIDE SOLILOQUIES』（U&R records）大好評発売中です。ボーカロイドを聴かない方でもぜひこの機会にチェックしてみてください。
Illustrates in a modern style, with a strong sense of direction woven into each piece. Collaboration with Orangestar has culminated in their first major album, *Mikansei Eight Beats* (Subcul-rise Record) and second major album, *SEASIDE SOLILOQUIES* (U&R records), both of which are now on sale and have been widely praised. Even for those who don't normally listen to Vocaloid music, this would be a great chance to check out these great albums.

T： Photoshop / CLIP STUDIO PAINT / シャープペンシル
Photoshop / CLIP STUDIO PAINT / mechanical pencil

くっか ｜ kukka

W：kukkakukka09.wixsite.com/kukka   **M**：kukkakukka09@gmail.com   **Tw**：@hamukukka

P：1995年9月29日生まれ。愛媛県出身。
Born on September 29, 1995 and hailing from Ehime Prefecture, Japan

C：自分が見たものや感じたことを自分の世界観で表現したいと思っています。生物と人との絡み、和洋折衷や陰の中にある光を描くのが好きです。
I want to express the things I see and feel through my own unique world. Some of my favorite subjects to draw are the relationship between people and living things, the intersection between Japanese and Western styles, and light in the midst of shadows.

T： Photoshop / SAI2 / シャープペンシル
Photoshop / SAI2 / mechanical pencil

W = Website   **M** = E-mail   **Tw** = Twitter (Username)   **Pi** = pixiv (User ID)   **P** = Profile   **C** = Comment   **T** = Tool

155

黒須ノカ　|　Noka Kurosu

W：http://www.giostrak.2-d.jp　**M**：giostra.contact@gmail.com　**Tw**：@giostra_info

P：東京都出身、在住。都内百貨店にてＰＯＰデザイナーとして数年間勤務し、現在はファンタジー系の風景・背景イラスト制作を中心にフリーランスとして活動中。主にゲームの背景や書籍の挿絵、CD ジャケットイラスト等を制作しています。
Hails from Tokyo and still resides there. Worked for several years at a department store in the city designing POP displays. These days mainly does fantasy-style scenery and background illustrations as a freelancer. Focuses on video game scenery illustrations for publications, as well as CD jacket illustrations.

C：はじめまして、黒須と申します。あったらいいなと思う景色が浮かんだら、見る人にわかりやすいように、スクリーンに映し出すつもりで作品を制作しています。この場所に行きたい、実際に見てみたいと感じていただけましたら、とても嬉しいです。
Hi, I'm Kurosu. When I have an image in my head of some scenery I like, I do illustrations to try to project that image to people through the screen so they can get a clear picture. If I can give people the feeling that they want to actually go to the place in the picture, or that they want to see the place with their own eyes, that would really make me happy.

T：Photoshop CS5 / SAI

K,Kanehira

W：http://k-kanehira.tumblr.com　**M**：k_kanehira_fi@ybb.ne.jp

P：フリーの背景デザイナー（アニメの美術設定・コンセプト画など）。趣味でもイラストを描いています。近代建築や生活美の感じられる街並みやつちのこをこよなく愛しています。
I'm a freelance scenery designer by trade (background artist, concept artist, etc. for anime), and I also do illustration as a hobby. I have great love for modern architecture, cityscapes that capture the beauty of daily life, and tsuchinoko creatures.

T：Photoshop CS5 / シャープペンシル
Photoshop CS5 / mechanical pencil

けみ猫　|　kemineko

W：http://kemineko.tumblr.com　**M**：kemineko@hotmail.co.jp　**Tw**：@kemineko　**Pi**：864706

P：5 月 28 日生まれ。神戸市在住。
Born on May 28 and currently resides in Kobe, Japan.

C：空想世界「エソラニア」を舞台にファンタジーな風景画を描いております、どうぞよろしくお願いします。
I draw fantasy landscape scenes from my own imaginary world of Esorania.
Thank you for checking out my art.

T：Photoshop CS5 / CLIP STUDIO PAINT

Kenta Doi

W：http://rosenfield.wixsite.com/nazfa

P：10 月 20 日生まれ。東京都八丈島出身。ゲームなどのコンセプトアート、イラスト、マットペイント、背景のお仕事をしています。
From Tokyo's Hachijo-jima Island. Born on October 20. Currently does concept art for video games and the like, in addition to illustration, matte painting and other scenery-related work.

C：応援よろしくお願いします。
Thank you for your support.

T：Photoshop CC

防人　|　sakimori

Tw：@sakimori_st30　**Pi**：211515

P：1986 年生まれ。神奈川県出身。主な活動経歴に『レムリアの女神』（大橋崇行著、未知谷）、『鳥居の向こうは、知らない世界でした。 癒しの薬園と仙人の師匠』（友麻 碧 著、幻冬舎文庫）の装画やブラウザ・ソーシャルゲームの背景などがある。
Born in 1986 and hailing from Kanagawa Prefecture, Japan. Career highlights include book cover illustrations for *Remuria no Megami* (Written by Takayuki Ohashi, Publisher Michitani), *Torii no Mukou wa Shiranai Sekai Deshita. Iyashi no Yakuen to Sennin no Shishou* (Written by Midori Yuma, Gentosha Bunko), as well as scenery illustrations for browser and social games.

C：風景画をメインに描いていますが、抽象的な絵や人物画などいろいろな絵を描けるよう勉強中。空と猫耳とヘッドホンが大好物です。
I mainly draw scenery illustrations, but also do some other art like abstract illustrations, portraits and the like as I study towards being able to draw a wide variety of subjects. My favorite things are the sky, cat's ears and headphones.

T：SAI

澤井富士彦　|　FUJIHIKO SAWAI

M：fujihiko.sawai@gmail.com　**Pi**：264261

P：コンセプトアーティスト、デザイナー（フリーランス）。1987 年 5 月 7 日生まれ。静岡県出身。学生時代のアルバイトで、アニメ制作会社の背景 CG 制作を経験。ゲーム会社でキャラクターモデラーとして活動した後、フリーランスのコンセプトアーティストとして映画やコンシューマゲーム（AAA タイトル）の背景コンセプトアートや設定画、アニメ、映像のイメージボード制作、PC ゲームのプロップ武器デザインや背景、モンスターイラスト、キャラクターデザインなどを手掛けています。
Concept artist and designer (freelance). Born on May 7, 1987 and comes from Shizuoka Prefecture, Japan. Did scenery CG for an anime company as a part time job while attending school. After working as a character modeler for a video game company, began work as a freelance concept artist for media such as movies and video games (AAA titles) doing scenery concept art and character set images, image board creation for anime and videos, weapon prop design and scenery design for PC games, monster illustrations, as well as character design.

C：普段自分の絵がこのようなかたちで掲載される事はあまりないため、読者の皆様に自分の作品を観ていただける機会を得られたこと、絵描きを生業としている者として大変光栄に思います。少しでも観ていただける方にワクワクや感動を与えられるような絵が描けるよう精進して参ります。
My illustrations are not normally featured in publications like this, so for readers to have the chance to check out my work is a tremendous honor for me as an artist. I'll concentrate on continuing to produce art that moves and excites the people who see it.

T：Photoshop CC / Maya / ZBrush 等

四季まこと　|　Makoto Shiki

W：http://makkou4ri.wixsite.com/bajo-shonen-sugu　http://makkou4.deviantart.com
M：makkou4ri@gmail.com　**Tw**：@makkou_4　**Pi**：10160

P：フリーランスのイラストレーター・デザイナーとしてファンタジー・SF ジャンルを中心に、コンセプトアート・背景・キャラクター・クリーチャーなどを制作。ゲーム・書籍など幅広いジャンルでのお仕事を募集中。
Active as a freelance illustrator and designer focusing on fantasy and science fiction. Creates concept art, scenery, characters and creatures, and is interested in taking on new work in a variety of genres, such as games or publications.

C：イラストレーターとして活動しております、四季まことと申します。商業で絵の仕事に携わる傍ら、個人でも創作活動に励んでおります。今回掲載していただいた作品のモチーフはさまざまですが、普段は草原を舞台に民族調のモチーフを散りばめたファンタジーの世界を描くことが多いです。私の作品を通じて幻想の世界の歴史、文化、大自然、何よりもそんな世界に生きる人々の心に想いを馳せていただけますと幸いです。
My name is Makoto Shiki and I work as an illustrator. Though art is part of my job, I also create on the side, in my own time. The pictures included in this publication follow several different motifs, but for the most part I tend to draw grassy surroundings inlaid with ethnic-themed motifs set in a fantasy world. Through my work, I would be very happy for you to get a real sense of the imaginary world's history, culture and natural beauty, but even more than that I'd like you to be able to feel the emotions of the people living there.

T：Photoshop CC2017 / Painter2018 / Illustrator CS6 / CLIP STUDIO PAINT

JohnHathway

W：http://mots.jp　**M**：info@mots.jp　**Tw**：@JohnHathway

P：少年時代に想像した反重力の世界を実現すべく物理学の研究者となった後に表現者ともなり、絵画、ロボット、小説、装置、ソフトウェアなどのテクノロジーと世界観を融合させた作品群を創出。最近はロボットと彫刻の中間物「Δ-Figure」（アルスエレクトロニカ 2014）や同氏の世界観ゲームアプリ「真空管ドールズ」、乗物型作品「MOVER」（神戸ビエンナーレ 2015）などの作品を発表、2016 年はスーパーフラットの潮流の展示である「Juxtapoz x Superflat 展」に日本代表アーティストの 1 人として海外展示を行った。2017 年は秋葉原の駅前の「秋葉原ラジオ会館」に 20m 級の巨大壁画作品や「Yahoo! JAPAN」に縦 30 万ピクセル超の巨大 CG 作品を公開した。
He became an expressive person after becoming a researcher in physics to realize the world of anti-gravity that he dreamed of as a child, leading him to create many works that combined technology with his world view, including drawings, robots, novels, devices, and software. He has recently presented *Δ-Figure* (Ars Electronica, 2014), a robot-sculpture hybrid, *Shinkukan Dolls*, a game app with his worldview, and *MOVER* (Kobe Biennale, 2015), a vehicle-shaped art piece. He was one of the Japanese artists to present at Juxtapoz x Superflat in 2016, an international exhibition that features the superflat trend in art. In 2017, his enormous 20-meter mural was displayed on the Akihabara Radiokaikan Building in front of Akihabara Station and an extremely large CG work with a height of over 300,000 pixels was released on Yahoo! JAPAN.

C：科学とオタクとアートのはざまの表現を追求しております。
My goal is to find a way to express the interval between science, otaku culture, and art.

T：Photoshop CC

shirakaba

W：http://bonenod.com　**M**：bonenod@gmail.com

P：1986 年生まれ。書籍装画、コンセプトアート等を中心に制作しています。
Born in 1986. Mainly designs things like concept art and cover illustrations for publications.

C：SF 的な世界観が好きで描いています。掲載作品のように景観を主題にする他、キャラクターイラストなど幅広く制作しています。
My love of science fiction keeps me drawing. I draw landscapes, such as those included in this book, but I also do character illustrations and a wide variety of other material.

T：Photoshop CS5 / CLIP STUDIO PAINT

彗　|　Sui

W：http://suiseistarcomet.ame-zaiku.com　**M**：suiseicomet@yahoo.co.jp

P：主にカードゲームやアプリのイラスト、コンセプトイメージ等、商業での制作を中心に活動しています。
Does illustrations for things like card games and mobile applications, as well as concept images, with a main focus on illustrations for commercial use.

C：ファンタジーな世界観やキャラクターが大好きでよく描いています。
I love fantasy worlds and their characters, so those are what I often draw.

T：SAI2

禅之助　|　zennosuke

M：rakugaki300page@gmail.com　**Tw**：@rakugaki100page

P：1992 年 10 月 2 日生まれ。書籍の装画、宣伝イラスト等を描かせていただいております。主な活動経歴は『かがみの孤城』（辻村深月 著、ポプラ社）、文庫版『天盆』（王城夕紀 著、中央公論新社）の装画等。
Born on October 2, 1992. Does illustrations for book covers, advertisements and the like. Major work includes a cover illustrations for *Kagami no Kojo* (Written by Mizuki Tsujimura, POPLAR Publishing Co., Ltd.), and *Tembon* (Written by Yuki Ojo, CHUOKORON-SHINSHA, Inc.) Paperback Edition.

C：イラストを見ていただき、ありがとうございます。自分もこんな絵描いてみたいと思っていただければ幸いです。
Thank you for looking at my illustrations. I think it would be great if you saw these and got the motivation to draw the same kind of thing yourself.

T：Krita

Soraizumi

M：KleinesGluckChrome@me.com　**Tw**：@KleinesGluck　**Pi**：6559742

P：1977 年 12 月 19 日生まれ。北海道出身。キャラクターデザイン、Web デザイン、UI 制作などを広く浅く。現在はゲーム関連会社のイラストレーターとして勤務しています。
Born on December 19, 1977 in Hokkaido. Character design, web design, UI creation and more; a little bit of everything. Currently working as an illustrator for a video game company.

C：ご覧いただき、ありがとうございます。Soraizumi と申します。好き勝手に描きたいものを盛り込みつつ、見ていただいた方が作品の世界に入り込めるような臨場感あるイラストを目指しています。
Thank you for checking out my work. I'm Soraizumi. I basically draw whatever I please, but I'm aiming for illustrations with a sense of presence that draw the viewer into the world.

T：CLIP STUDIO PAINT PRO

そらは | soraha

Tw：@owlforest0   **Pi**：3162829

P：茨城県出身。主にファンタジーの風景イラストを制作しています。空や宇宙などのモチーフが好きです。
From Ibaraki Prefecture, Japan. Creates mostly fantasy-style illustrations. Favorite motifs are the sky and outer space.

C：今回掲載していただいたイラストは、空と海が融合したような不思議な世界をテーマにして描いたものです。いろいろなファンタジーの世界を想像するのが好きで、幻想的な雰囲気や広がりのある絵を意識して描いています。
The pictures I've included here were drawn with the theme of a marvelously unique world in which sea and sky are one in the same. I really enjoy dreaming up all kinds of fantastic worlds, and I try to draw illustrations with a magical feel that seem to be wide open.

T：Photoshop CS5 / Cintiq 27QHD

高原聡史 | Satoshi Takahara

W：https://www.artstation.com/artist/satoshi-takahara
M：takahara.art@gmail.com   **Tw**：@ART_Takahara   **Pi**：9820913

P：1993 年 7 月 23 日生まれ。埼玉県出身。2016 年、早稲田大学創造理工学部建築学科卒業。映画やアニメ、ゲームなどのコンセプトアートやデザインを中心に活動中。主な参加作品は、映画『バイオハザード ヴェンデッタ』、TV アニメ『こねこのチー』、VR ゲーム『ハネチャリ』等のコンセプトアート・デザイン。
Born on July 23, 1993 and hailing from Saitama Prefecture, Japan. Graduated from Waseda University's School of Creative Science and Engineering, Department of Architecture in 2016. Now mainly focuses on concept art and design for movies, anime and video games. The major pieces I worked on were concept art and designs for the film *Resident Evil: Vendetta*, the TV anime *Koneko no Chi*, and the VR game *Hanechari*.

C：作品を見ていただいてありがとうございます！ まだまだ未熟者ですが、立ち止まらずに挑戦し続けていきたいです！ 今年は CG とキャラクターを頑張るつもりです！よろしくお願いします！
Thank you for taking a look at my work! I'm still just a beginner, but I plan to keep challenging myself and I won't give up! This year I want to do my best with CG and characters! I appreciate your support!

T：Photoshop CC / ZBrush4R7 / KeyShot

たみ。 | Tami

M：neko_neto@yahoo.co.jp   **Pi**：107492

P：東京都在住。主に背景を描きます。世界観や設定を作るのが得意です。
Resides in the greater Tokyo area and mostly draws scenery illustrations. Highly skilled at creating settings and conveying the sense of being in another world.

C：「こんな場所に行ってみたい！」と思ってもらえるような世界観を大切にしています。見てくれた人がワクワクするような、そんな背景を目指しています。
The sense of looking into another world and thinking, "I'd like to visit a place like this!" is what I want people to experience when they see my work. I aim to draw scenery that excites the people who see it.

T：Photoshop CS6 / つけペン
Photoshop CS6 / dip pen

電鬼 | Denki

W：http://fusionfactory.fc2web.com   **M**：denki0917@hotmail.co.jp

P：主な活動経歴に『Z/X -Zillions of enemy X-』（BROCCOLI / Nippon Ichi Software, inc.）、『ラクエンロジック』（ブシロード）、『LORD of VERMILION III』（スクウェア・エニックス）カードイラスト、コンシューマーゲームの背景グラフィック制作など。
Major works include card illustrations for *Z/X -Zillions of enemy X-* (BROCCOLI / Nippon Ichi Software, inc.), *Luck & Logic* (Bushiroad) and *LORD of VERMILION III* (SQUARE ENIX), and design of scenery graphics for consumer games.

C：背景と女の子をよく描きます。厚塗りを中心としたイラストを描きます。
As subjects I mostly draw girls and scenery, and recently have been doing illustrations with a thick painting style.

T：Photoshop CC / CLIP STUDIO PAINT

友野るい | Rui Tomono

M：pulupulu_gene@yahoo.co.jp   **Pi**：27526

P：コンセプトアート、イメージボード、イラストの分野で活動しております。主な活動経歴は『ZERO ESCAPE 刻のジレンマ』（Spike Chunsoft Co., Ltd.）、『EARTH WARS』（oneoreight）のキャラクターデザインなど。
I mostly work with concept art, image boards and illustration. A couple of the big projects I've worked on are character designs for *Zero Time Dilemma* (Spike Chunsoft Co., Ltd.) and *EARTH WARS* (oneoreight).

C：SNS でも活動をしているので、製品化されたもの以外の絵などもそちらでご覧いただけたら幸いです。
I'm also active on SNS, so I'd be happy for you to look for me there, where you might have a chance to see some of my artwork that is not put into final products.

T：Photoshop CS5

nocras

W：http://nocras666.tumblr.com   **M**：bespin666@gmail.com

P：2 月 25 日生まれ。岐阜県出身。以前はゲーム会社にて 3D デザイナーをしていました。現在はフリーランスのコンシューマーゲームのコンセプトアーティストや、トレーディングカードゲームのイラストレーターとして活動しています。
Born on February 25 and comes from Gifu Prefecture, Japan. Previously worked as a 3D designer for a video game company. Currently works freelance as a concept artist for video games and as an illustrator for trading card games.

C：主にオリエンタルな世界観のイラストを描いています。独特なキャラクターデザインや存在感のある背景を見ていただけると幸いです。
I tend to draw worlds with an Asian feel. I hope you can enjoy the unique character design combined with the strong presence of the scenery.

T：Photoshop CC / SAI

PiNe

M：yellowpine112@gmail.com　**Tw**：@PiNe11298　**Pi**：5403033

P：1998 年生まれ。
Born in 1998.

C：子どもの頃から憧れている現実とファンタジーを掛け合わせたような世界観、情景をよく描いています。
I enjoy drawing the kinds of images I've loved since I was a kid, especially scenes that show a world with fantasy and reality mixed together.

T：Photoshop CC2015 / Procreate

藤木ゆう ｜ Yu Fujiki

M：you.fujiki@gmail.com　**Tw**：@fujiki_you

P：1989 年 9 月 11 日生まれ。福岡県出身。18 歳の時に少年誌の漫画家としてデビュー。22 歳から 2 年間フリーランスのイラストレーターとして活動後、現在はゲーム会社でイラストレーター、デザイナーとして活動中。
Born on September 11, 1989 and comes from Fukuoka Prefecture, Japan. Debuted at the age of 18 as a manga artist for a shounen manga magazine. Worked for two years as a freelance illustrator from the age of 22, before switching to current role as an illustrator and designer for a video game company.

C：イラストレーターとして仕事を始めて 1、2 年目の頃の作品になります。昔から有機物と無機質の融合をテーマに絵を描く事が多く、廃墟やスチームパンクの世界観が大好きです。これからもわくわく、ぞくぞくするようないろいろな世界を描いていきたいです。
These illustrations are from my first two years working as an illustrator. One of the major themes I've been drawing for a long time is the fusion of organic and inorganic matter, and I really like ancient ruins and steampunk-inspired settings. I want to keep drawing all kinds of different, exciting and spine-tingling worlds.

T：Photoshop CS6

藤ちょこ ｜ fuzichoco

W：http://www.fuzichoco.com　**M**：fuzichoko@yahoo.co.jp

P：9 月 30 日生まれ。千葉県出身、東京都在住のイラストレーター。ライトノベルやトレーディングカードゲーム、ソーシャルゲーム等のイラストを中心に活動しています。
Born on September 30. Currently lives in Tokyo but originally comes from Chiba Prefecture, Japan. Mostly does illustrations for light novels, trading card games, social network games and the like.

C：ファンタジーな風景は見るのも描くのも好きなので、本書に呼んでいただけてとても光栄です。
I enjoy both looking at and drawing fantasy scenery, so being asked to submit my work for this book was a big honor for me.

T：Photoshop CS5 / CLIP STUDIO PAINT / openCanvas6

実田くら ｜ mita kura

M：taisyaku@live.jp

P：福島県在住。フリーのイラストレーター。カードイラストやゲームの背景などを中心に制作しております。ファンタジックな風景が好き。
Currently resides in Fukushima Prefecture, Japan. Freelance Illustrator. Designs illustrations for card games and scenery for video games. Loves fanciful, fantasy style settings.

C：ほとんどの絵に共通の文字や物が隠れています。ぜひ見つけてみてください！
In most of my drawings there are hidden letters or items. Try to find them if you can!

T：Photoshop CS5 / つけペン / インク / 鉛筆
Photoshop CS5 / dip pen / ink / pencil

もの久保 ｜ Monokubo

W：http://ariduka55.tumblr.com　**M**：1303ariduka@gmail.com　**Tw**：@13033303　**Pi**：4545042

P：1994 年 10 月 30 日生まれ。静岡県出身。主な活動経歴に『バトルスピリッツ』（バンダイ）などがある。
Originally from Shizuoka Prefecture, Japan and was born on October 30, 1994. Career history includes work on the *Battle Spirits* (BANDAI) trading card game and others.

C：本書をご覧いただき、大変光栄です。Twitter 等でいつも見てくださっている方はありがとうございます。自然の風景を描くときが一番楽しく、心が癒されます。雪とか岩とか葉っぱとか最高ですよね。
I feel very honored to be included in this book and to have you check out my illustrations. I'd like to say thank you to everyone who follows me and looks at my posts on Twitter and other social media. Drawing natural settings is the most fun for me, and that's what really eases my mind. Snow, rocks and leaves are the best, aren't they?

T：Photoshop CC

よー清水 ｜ Yo Shimizu

W：：http://xpxjp218.wix.com/yo-shimizu　**M**：yo.shimizu629@gmail.com　**Tw**：@you629　**Pi**：2830609

P：大学卒業後、イラストレーター、コンセプトアーティストとして活動。『甲鉄城のカバネリ』コンセプトアート、Adobe Photoshop 公式イラスト、PlayStation4、PlayStation Vita、ニンテンドー 3DS などのコンシューマーゲームやスマートフォンゲームの背景画、書籍の装画、カードイラスト、デジタルペインティングの講演など幅広く活動している。著書に『「ファンタジー背景」描き方教室』（SB クリエイティブ）がある。
Graduate from university and currently works as an illustrator and concept artist. Diverse range of work that includes illustrating concept art for *Kabaneri of the Iron Fortress*, creating illustrations for the Adobe Photoshop official website, scenery art for both consumer games such as for PlayStation4, PlayStation Vita, and Nintendo 3DS, and smartphone games, book covers, card illustrations, and giving lectures on digital painting, as well as a published book, *'Fantaji Haikei' Kakikata Kyoushitsu* (SB Creative).

C：その場の空気感や匂いを感じられるような作品を目指しています。
My goal is to create illustrations that evoke details like the overall atmosphere and even the smell of the place depicted.

T：Photoshop CC2017 / CLIP STUDIO PAINT

W = Website   **M** = E-mail   **Tw** = Twitter (Username)   **Pi** = pixiv (User ID)   **P** = Profile   **C** = Comment   **T** = Tool

159

礼 心　｜　Reishin

W： http://reishin.blog.shinobi.jp　**M：** starstar.river@gmail.com

P： 1984 年、千葉県生まれ。アニメ背景の会社を経て、現在はコンセプトアートの仕事を中心に活動しています。
Born in Chiba Prefecture, Japan in 1984. Worked for an anime scenery art company in the past and currently produces mostly concept art.

C： 大人も見られるファンタジーを目指しています。ひと時の夢の世界をご堪能ください。
My goal is to create fantasy that adults can enjoy. I'd like you to be able to admire a dream world captured in a moment.

T： Photoshop CS5

わ い っ し ゅ　｜　yish

M： yyish.yy@gmail.com　**Tw：** @yyish　**Pi：** 4147414

P： 1983 年生まれ。愛知県出身。主に背景・環境アーティストとして活動している。イラストメイキングを公開するなど SNS でも積極的に活動している。
Born in 1983 and hailing from Aichi Prefecture, Japan. Does scenery and environmental illustrations. Participates actively in SNS, sharing things like "Illustration Making," a series of how-to articles about the illustration process with followers.

C： 絵の世界に入り込めるような、そんな作品を目指しています。世界観を楽しんでいただけたら嬉しく思います。
My goal is to draw pictures that you feel like you could step into at any moment. I'd be very pleased if my work allowed you experience the feeling of being in a new world.

T： Photoshop CC / CLIP STUDIO PAINT

美しい情景イラストレーション
ファンタジー編
幻想的な風景を描くクリエイターズファイル

Beautiful Scenes from a Fantasy World:
Background Illustrations and Scenes from Anime and Manga Works

2017 年 9 月 13 日　初版第 1 刷発行
2020 年 12 月 10 日　　　第 4 刷発行

編著
パイ インターナショナル

カバーイラスト
よー清水

装丁・本文デザイン
杉山峻輔

翻訳
Matthew Forrest
ブレインウッズ株式会社

編集協力
井上綾乃

編集
杵淵恵子

協力
NBC ユニバーサル・エンターテイメントジャパン
おさむらいさん
ソニー・ミュージックエンタテインメント
SB クリエイティブ
つばさレコーズ
専門学校日本マンガ芸術学院
ビー・エヌ・エヌ新社
マイクロマガジン社
yucat　http://www.yucat1031.com

発行人
三芳寛要

発行元
株式会社 パイ インターナショナル
〒170-0005
東京都豊島区南大塚 2-32-4
TEL 03-3944-3981
FAX 03-5395-4830
sales@pie.co.jp

印刷・製本
株式会社廣済堂